INVISIBLE ASSETS AND LIABILITIES

A Retirement Resilience Book

Mridul Joshi

Build What Compounds in Your Favor.
Eliminate What Compounds Against You.

Amba Bhavan Publications
Orlando, Florida

First Edition
2026

Title:
Invisible Assets and Liabilities: A Retirement Resilience Book

Author:
Mridul Joshi

Paperback ISBN:
979-8-9930198-7-1

Hardcover ISBN:
979-8-9930198-6-4

Disclaimer

This book is intended for educational and informational purposes only. The author is not providing financial, legal, tax, investment, medical, or professional advice. Readers should consult qualified professionals regarding their individual circumstances.

The views, experiences, and examples presented in this book are those of the author and are intended to illustrate concepts related to retirement resilience, invisible assets, invisible liabilities, and personal decision-making.

Publisher:
Amba Bhavan Publications
Orlando, Florida, USA

Contents

Introduction

Retirement is often presented as a financial destination defined by savings, investments, and net worth. While these visible measures are important, they tell only part of the story. Over time I came to realize that many of the factors that most strongly influence the quality of retirement cannot be found on a balance sheet.

This book introduces a broader framework built around two complementary ideas: Invisible Assets and Invisible Liabilities. Invisible Assets—such as health, relationships, knowledge, experience, travel, spirituality, time, freedom, and reliable income—compound in your favor. Invisible Liabilities—such as poor health, isolation, chronic stress, unmanaged debt, fear, wasted time, and unnecessary churn—compound against you.

Retirement resilience is created not merely by accumulating financial wealth, but by strengthening the invisible assets that enrich life while steadily reducing the invisible liabilities that erode freedom. Every chapter in this book can therefore be viewed through two simple questions:

- Which Invisible Asset is being strengthened?
- Which Invisible Liability is being reduced?

This is not a book about achieving a perfect retirement. Rather, it is about building a resilient life—one capable of adapting to uncertainty while preserving meaning, purpose, and freedom. Throughout the book you will find reflections, worksheets, and practical examples intended to help you evaluate your own Hidden Portfolio and identify opportunities for steady improvement.

Although the discussion is centered on retirement, the underlying principles apply throughout life. The habits, relationships, perspectives, and decisions that compound over decades ultimately shape not only our retirement years but also our resilience, our legacy, and our peace of mind.

My hope is that this framework encourages you to look beyond traditional measures of wealth, recognize the invisible assets you already possess, strengthen those that can still grow, and thoughtfully reduce the invisible liabilities that stand in their way. If it helps you preserve freedom, reduce regret, and live with greater resilience, then this book will have fulfilled its purpose.

Chapter 1 – The Invisible Assets

When most people think about retirement, they think about money. Over time, I came to realize that some of the most valuable assets in retirement do not appear on any financial statement. I call these Invisible Assets.

The first invisible asset I recognized was Social Security. Later I realized that health, mobility, relationships, knowledge, purpose, travel, spiritual perspective, and time itself are also powerful retirement assets.

Invisible Assets include:
- Financial Security
- Health Capital
- Relationship Capital
- Knowledge Capital
- Experience Capital
- Spiritual Capital
- Time Capital
- Freedom Capital

Case Study:
Imagine two retirees. One has substantial financial wealth but poor health and limited purpose. The other has modest savings, good health, meaningful relationships, daily activity, and inflation-protected income. Traditional accounting may favor the first retiree. Retirement resilience may favor the second.

Worksheet:
1. List three invisible assets you possess.

2. Which contributes most to your quality of life?
3. Which needs the most improvement?
4. What action will you take in the next year?

The purpose of this book is to help readers recognize, develop, and protect the invisible assets that create a resilient life.

Chapter 2 - Invisible Liabilities: The Other Half of the Hidden Portfolio

Most retirement planning emphasizes building assets. This book proposes that retirement resilience depends upon two complementary disciplines: building Invisible Assets while simultaneously recognizing, managing, and reducing Invisible Liabilities. Invisible Assets compound in your favor. Invisible Liabilities compound against you.

What Are Invisible Liabilities?

Most financial planning identifies visible liabilities such as mortgages, credit-card balances, and other debt. This book proposes that many of the greatest threats to retirement resilience are largely invisible. They seldom appear on a balance sheet, yet they quietly erode freedom, health, peace of mind, adaptability, and quality of life.

Examples of Invisible Liabilities

Poor health and declining functional capacity

Isolation and loneliness

Chronic stress and anxiety

Lack of purpose

Fear and excessive uncertainty

Inflexibility and inability to adapt

Knowledge stagnation

Neglected relationships

Misallocation of time

Decision fatigue and unnecessary churn

Inflation vulnerability

Debt that limits future freedom

Attachment to outcomes rather than right action

Passive living and accumulating future regrets

The Two-Sided Retirement Balance Sheet

Every retiree manages two simultaneous processes:

Build Invisible Assets.

Reduce Invisible Liabilities.

Retirement resilience grows when assets compound faster than liabilities.

How This Book Is Organized

Each chapter can be viewed through two complementary questions:

Which Invisible Asset is being strengthened?

Which Invisible Liability is being reduced or prevented?

For example, Health Assets counter poor health; Relationship Assets counter isolation; Knowledge Assets counter stagnation; Spiritual Assets reduce fear and attachment to outcomes; Time Assets counter wasted time; Freedom Assets reduce unnecessary constraints;

and the chapters on Debt in Context and the Churn Principle examine important Invisible Liabilities directly.

The Central Thesis

Retirement resilience is not determined solely by the assets we accumulate. It is equally influenced by the liabilities we allow to compound. A resilient life therefore requires two complementary disciplines: build what compounds in your favor and eliminate what compounds against you.

Reflection

Throughout the chapters that follow, consider every idea through this lens:

Does this strengthen an Invisible Asset?

Does this reduce an Invisible Liability?

That simple framework provides a practical way to evaluate choices throughout retirement and, more broadly, throughout life.

Chapter 3 – Social Security: The Foundational Invisible Asset

When I first began thinking seriously about retirement, I looked at the usual numbers. Savings. Investments. Debt. Income. Net worth. Like many people, I focused on what could be seen.

Yet one of the most important assets in my retirement had been quietly growing in the background for decades.

That asset was Social Security.

I now view Social Security as the foundational invisible asset. It is not invisible because it is secret.
It is invisible because many people underestimate its value. They see a monthly payment but fail to see the larger structure behind it: inflation protection, longevity insurance, survivor protection, and a reliable income stream that continues regardless of market volatility.

In my own retirement journey, I came to appreciate that a larger Social Security benefit creates something far more important than additional income. It creates resilience.

A larger benefit can help pay the electric bill during

inflationary periods. It can help cover medical expenses. It can reduce the need to liquidate investments during market downturns. Most importantly, it can provide peace of mind.

EXAMPLE

Imagine two retirees.

Retiree A receives $1,500 per month from Social Security.
Retiree B receives $3,500 per month.

Both receive annual cost-of-living adjustments.

Over time, the larger benefit not only produces more income but also creates a larger inflation-adjusted foundation. The difference compounds year after year.

I call this creating a bigger base.

The larger the base, the larger the canvas upon which retirement can be lived.

MY LESSON

Over time I realized that retirement is not simply about maximizing assets. It is about creating enough reliable income to support freedom, flexibility, and resilience.

WORKSHEET

1. What is your current estimated Social Security benefit?

2. Have you reviewed your earnings record?
3. What actions could increase your future benefit?
4. How would an additional $500 per month change your retirement lifestyle?
5. What would greater income certainty mean to your peace of mind?

REFLECTION

Social Security is not the only invisible asset. But for many Americans it is the first invisible asset, the foundation upon which many other invisible assets can flourish.

Health, relationships, travel, learning, purpose, and freedom are all easier to cultivate when a stable financial foundation exists.

That is why Social Security earns its place as the foundational invisible asset in this book.

Chapter 4 – Health Assets: The Wealth You Carry Within You

When most people hear the word wealth, they think of money. I certainly did.

Yet retirement taught me a lesson that no financial statement could adequately capture. The ability to walk, breathe comfortably, climb a flight of stairs, travel, learn, and enjoy a sunrise may ultimately be worth more than a larger investment account.

Health is one of the most powerful invisible assets.

Unlike money, health is experienced directly every day. It influences energy, mobility, confidence, independence, and quality of life.

I began to appreciate this truth more deeply as I grew older. The older we become, the more health reveals its value. A retiree with modest savings and excellent functional health may enjoy a richer retirement than someone with a much larger portfolio but severe limitations.

THE DIFFERENCE BETWEEN HEALTH AND HEALTH CAPITAL

Health is your current condition.

Health Capital is the accumulated result of years of choices.

Every walk, every meal, every hour of sleep, every medical appointment, every effort to reduce stress contributes to Health Capital.

Like financial capital, Health Capital compounds.

CASE STUDY

Imagine two retirees at age seventy.

The first has accumulated a substantial portfolio but rarely exercises and has neglected preventive care.

The second has a smaller portfolio but remains physically active, maintains social connections, walks daily, and continues to learn and explore.

Ten years later the difference may be dramatic.

The second retiree may possess greater freedom despite possessing less money.

THE FREEDOM CONNECTION

Health creates freedom.

Freedom to travel.
Freedom to visit family.
Freedom to volunteer.
Freedom to pursue hobbies.
Freedom to learn.

Freedom to serve.

Without health, many other invisible assets become difficult to enjoy.

MY PERSONAL OBSERVATION

Throughout retirement I discovered that maintaining functionality often mattered more than achieving athletic performance.

I did not need to become an elite athlete.

I simply needed to remain capable.

Capability became the goal.

WORKSHEET: HEALTH CAPITAL INVENTORY

Rate yourself from 1 to 10.

Physical Energy:
Mobility:
Strength:
Balance:
Sleep Quality:
Stress Management:
Preventive Care:
Nutrition:
Social Activity:
Sense of Purpose:

Which area needs the greatest improvement?

What one action can you begin this week?

THE COMPOUNDING EFFECT

A twenty-minute walk may seem insignificant.

Yet repeated over months and years, small actions create meaningful change.

Health Capital grows the same way retirement savings grow: one contribution at a time.

REFLECTION

Money can purchase many things.

It cannot purchase yesterday's health.

That is why Health Capital deserves recognition as one of the most important invisible assets in retirement.

For many retirees, protecting Health Capital may produce greater returns than pursuing additional financial gain.

Chapter 5 – Relationship Assets: The People Who Travel Through Life With You

When I was younger, I tended to think of success in individual terms.

Education.
Career.
Income.
Achievements.

As I moved deeper into retirement, I began to recognize a truth that is both simple and profound:

No one travels through life alone.

Relationships are among the most important invisible assets we possess.

Unlike financial assets, relationship assets cannot be measured on a brokerage statement.
Unlike real estate, they cannot be appraised.
Unlike investments, they cannot be purchased.

Yet they may be more valuable than all of those things combined.

THE HUMAN NETWORK

Every person carries an invisible network.

Family.
Friends.
Neighbors.
Mentors.
Teachers.
Faith communities.
Professional contacts.
Fellow travelers.

Some relationships last a season.
Others last a lifetime.

Together they form what I call Relationship Capital.

RELATIONSHIP CAPITAL

Relationship Capital is not measured by the number of people you know.

It is measured by the quality of connection.

A single trusted friend may be worth more than hundreds of casual acquaintances.

A strong family bond may provide greater security than a large financial reserve.

A caring neighbor may become invaluable during times of illness or crisis.

CASE STUDY

Imagine two retirees.

Retiree A has substantial financial resources but little social interaction.
Days pass without meaningful conversations.

Retiree B has a smaller portfolio but enjoys regular contact with family, friendships,
community activities, and social engagement.

Who possesses the stronger retirement foundation?

Financial planners often evaluate assets.

Retirement resilience requires evaluating relationships as well.

THE LONELINESS CHALLENGE

Many retirees discover that loneliness becomes a hidden risk.

Retirement can reduce daily interactions.
Children may live far away.
Friends relocate.
Health challenges limit activity.

Without intentional effort, Relationship Capital can slowly decline.

That decline may affect emotional health, physical health, and overall quality of life.

MY OBSERVATION

I have learned that meaningful conversations are a form of wealth.

Sharing ideas.
Helping others.
Receiving guidance.
Offering encouragement.

These experiences enrich life in ways that money cannot.

BUILDING RELATIONSHIP CAPITAL

Relationship Capital grows through deliberate investment.

Regular phone calls.
Shared meals.
Volunteer work.
Community involvement.
Religious participation.
Travel experiences.
Acts of service.

Like financial assets, relationships require maintenance.

WORKSHEET

Relationship Inventory

List five people who contribute positively to your life.

1.

2.
3.
4.
5.

Who have you not spoken with recently?

Which relationships would you like to strengthen?

What specific action can you take during the next month?

REFLECTION

Many invisible assets become stronger when shared.

Knowledge grows when taught.
Purpose grows when expressed.
Joy grows when shared.

Relationships create the environment in which many other invisible assets flourish.

Retirement is not simply about having enough money.

It is also about having people with whom to share the journey.

For that reason, Relationship Assets deserve a place among the most important invisible assets in retirement.

Chapter 6 – Knowledge Assets: The Wealth That Cannot Be Taken Away

Of all the invisible assets discussed in this book, Knowledge Capital may be the most portable.

Money can be lost.
Property can be damaged.
Markets can decline.
Careers can end.

Yet knowledge remains with us.

The older I become, the more I appreciate the value of accumulated knowledge. Some of that knowledge came through formal education. Much of it came through experience, mistakes, travel, conversations, reading, and observation.

Knowledge is not merely information.

Information tells us what happened.

Knowledge helps us understand why.

Wisdom helps us decide what to do next.

THE COMPOUNDING EFFECT OF KNOWLEDGE

Knowledge compounds.

Every book read builds upon previous books.

Every skill acquired makes future learning easier.

Every experience creates context for future decisions.

Unlike many assets, knowledge often becomes more valuable when shared.

THE RETIREMENT ADVANTAGE

Retirement provides something many people lacked during their working years:

Time to learn.

Many retirees rediscover curiosity.

They study history.
Learn languages.
Explore technology.
Read philosophy.
Research family history.
Develop artistic skills.

The process itself becomes rewarding.

CASE STUDY

Imagine two retirees.

Retiree A spends most days consuming passive entertainment.

Retiree B dedicates time to reading, learning, discussing ideas, and exploring new interests.

Ten years later, the differences may extend far beyond intellectual development.

Learning often creates purpose.

Purpose creates engagement.

Engagement supports resilience.

MY OBSERVATION

Some of the most interesting people I have met are lifelong learners.

Their curiosity did not end at retirement.

In many cases, retirement gave them the freedom to pursue subjects they had postponed for decades.

KNOWLEDGE AS AN ASSET CLASS

Knowledge Assets include:

- Professional expertise
- Life experience
- Technical skills
- Financial literacy
- Historical understanding
- Cultural awareness
- Spiritual understanding

- Problem-solving ability
- Communication skills

WORKSHEET

Knowledge Capital Inventory

What subjects interest you most?

What have you always wanted to learn?

What skills would improve your quality of life?

Which books would you like to read this year?

What educational goals would you like to pursue during retirement?

THE TEACHING EFFECT

One of the most powerful ways to strengthen Knowledge Capital is to teach.

Teaching forces us to clarify ideas.

It benefits both the student and the teacher.

Even informal mentoring creates value.

REFLECTION

The pursuit of knowledge is not merely an academic exercise.

It is a path toward growth, engagement, adaptability, and meaning.

Knowledge Capital expands opportunities.

It enriches conversations.

It deepens perspective.

Most importantly, it reminds us that retirement is not the end of growth.

It may be the beginning of a new phase of learning.

For these reasons, Knowledge Assets deserve recognition as one of the most valuable invisible assets in retirement.

Chapter 7 – Experience Assets: Building a Life Rich in Stories

When I was younger, I often measured progress using conventional markers.

Education.
Career advancement.
Income.
Home ownership.
Retirement savings.

These measurements have value, but over time I discovered that some of the richest forms of wealth do not
appear on financial statements.

They live in memory.

They live in experience.

They live in stories.

I call these Experience Assets.

THE VALUE OF EXPERIENCES

Experiences shape who we become.

A difficult challenge teaches resilience.

A journey broadens perspective.

A conversation changes understanding.

A setback builds character.

Unlike material possessions, experiences often become more valuable with time.

A purchased object may depreciate.

A meaningful experience may appreciate in significance for decades.

THE MEMORY DIVIDEND

One of the most remarkable qualities of Experience Assets is what I call the Memory Dividend.

An experience can continue paying benefits long after it occurs.

A family vacation may become a cherished memory.

A mountain climbed may become a source of confidence.

A volunteer project may create lifelong friendships.

A pilgrimage may deepen spiritual understanding.

The original event ends.

The benefits continue.

MY OBSERVATION

Looking back, some of the most valuable moments in my life were not the most expensive.

They were the experiences that expanded my perspective.

Traveling to unfamiliar places.
Meeting people from different cultures.
Learning new skills.
Facing unexpected challenges.

These experiences became part of my internal wealth.

CASE STUDY

Imagine two retirees.

Retiree A accumulates significant material possessions but rarely ventures beyond familiar routines.

Retiree B intentionally invests in meaningful experiences, learning opportunities, community activities,
travel, and personal growth.

At age eighty, whose memories create the richer internal landscape?

The answer may have little to do with financial net worth.

THE EXPERIENCE PORTFOLIO

Experience Assets may include:

- Travel adventures
- Volunteer work
- Family traditions
- Lifelong learning
- Spiritual journeys
- Creative pursuits
- Mentoring relationships
- Outdoor experiences
- Community service
- Personal achievements

THE COURAGE COMPONENT

Experience Assets often require courage.

Trying something new.
Visiting a new place.
Learning a difficult skill.
Meeting unfamiliar people.

Growth frequently occurs outside familiar routines.

THE REGRET TEST

A useful exercise is to imagine yourself twenty years into the future.

Which experiences would you regret not pursuing?

Which opportunities deserve action today?

Many retirees discover that delayed dreams become

sources of future regret.

WORKSHEET

Experience Asset Inventory

List five meaningful experiences from your life.

1.
2.
3.
4.
5.

What made them meaningful?

What experiences would you still like to pursue?

What is one experience you can begin planning during the next year?

THE STORY VALUE

Stories connect generations.

Experiences become stories.

Stories become legacy.

Children and grandchildren often remember stories long after financial details are forgotten.

The lessons embedded within experiences may become gifts to future generations.

REFLECTION

Financial security matters.

Health matters.

Relationships matter.

Yet life is also measured by experiences.

Experience Assets enrich retirement by creating perspective, meaning, gratitude, and memories.

For these reasons, Experience Assets deserve recognition as one of the most valuable invisible assets in retirement.

A life rich in stories is a form of wealth.

Chapter 8 – Travel Assets: Adventure, Perspective, and Renewal

When people discuss retirement planning, travel is often treated as an expense.

I view it differently.

Travel can be an investment.

Not necessarily an investment that produces financial returns, but an investment that generates perspective, growth, gratitude, memories, and renewal.

For that reason, I consider Travel Assets to be one of the most important invisible assets in retirement.

THE EXPANDING HORIZON

Travel expands horizons in ways that are difficult to achieve through books alone.

A photograph of a mountain is not the same as standing before it.

A documentary about another culture is not the same as sharing a meal with local residents.

Reading about a pilgrimage is not the same as walking the path yourself.

Travel transforms information into experience.

FROM TOURISM TO TRANSFORMATION

Not all travel creates Travel Assets.

Some travel is consumption.

Other travel is transformation.

Transformational travel changes how we see ourselves and the world.

It introduces uncertainty, adaptation, and discovery.

It reminds us that our familiar routines are only one way of living.

MY OBSERVATION

Some of the most meaningful experiences of my life occurred while traveling.

Travel exposed me to different cultures, beliefs, landscapes, and ways of thinking.

It created memories that continue to influence my perspective years later.

The financial cost of those journeys ended long ago.

The benefits continue.

THE PERSPECTIVE DIVIDEND

One of travel's greatest gifts is perspective.

Travel often reveals how much of life we take for granted.

It increases gratitude.

It encourages humility.

It broadens understanding.

Perspective itself becomes an invisible asset.

CASE STUDY

Imagine two retirees.

Retiree A remains almost entirely within familiar routines and environments.

Retiree B intentionally seeks new experiences through travel, exploration, and cultural discovery.

Over time, the second retiree may develop a broader understanding of people, places, and possibilities.

The journey becomes part of the retirement portfolio.

TRAVEL AS THERAPY

Travel can also function as a form of renewal.

A change of environment often refreshes the mind.

Nature reduces stress.

Pilgrimages encourage reflection.

Adventure promotes engagement.

The combination creates what I call the Renewal Dividend.

The trip ends.

The renewed perspective remains.

TYPES OF TRAVEL ASSETS

Travel Assets may include:

- Pilgrimages
- Family travel
- Cultural exploration
- Historical journeys
- Nature experiences
- Educational travel
- Volunteer travel
- International travel
- Local exploration
- Spiritual journeys

WORKSHEET

Travel Asset Inventory

What journeys have influenced your life most deeply?

1.
2.
3.
4.
5.

What lessons did those journeys teach?

What destination continues to call to you?

What travel experience would you regret not pursuing?

How can you begin planning it?

THE ACCESSIBILITY PRINCIPLE

Travel Assets do not require expensive international trips.

A nearby park can create renewal.

A local museum can create learning.

A short road trip can create memories.

The value lies not in distance traveled but in perspective gained.

REFLECTION

Travel enriches retirement by expanding perspective, creating memories, and renewing the spirit.

Experiences fade into stories.

Stories become wisdom.

Wisdom becomes part of who we are.

For these reasons, Travel Assets deserve recognition as one of the most powerful invisible assets available to retirees.

A well-lived retirement is often measured not merely by what we owned, but by where we went, what we learned, and who we became along the way.

Chapter 9 – Spiritual Assets: Meaning, Meditation, and Inner Peace

Of all the invisible assets discussed in this book, Spiritual Assets may be the most difficult to measure.

Yet they may also be among the most important.

Money can create comfort.

Health can create capability.

Relationships can create connection.

Knowledge can create understanding.

But spiritual assets help answer a different question:

Why?

Why am I here?
What gives life meaning?
How should I respond to success and failure?
What truly matters?

These questions become increasingly important as we grow older.

THE SEARCH FOR MEANING

Many people spend the first half of life building careers, raising families, and meeting obligations.

Retirement often creates space for reflection.

Without the constant demands of work, deeper questions emerge.

Some people discover new interests.

Others return to spiritual traditions they had neglected.

Many begin searching for meaning beyond achievement.

THE INNER PORTFOLIO

I think of Spiritual Assets as part of an Inner Portfolio.

Unlike financial assets, this portfolio exists entirely within us.

It includes:

- Faith
- Gratitude
- Compassion
- Forgiveness
- Wisdom
- Meditation
- Reflection
- Purpose
- Equanimity

• Dharma

These assets influence how we experience life regardless of external circumstances.

THE BHAGAVAD GITA

One spiritual teaching that has influenced my thinking is found in the Bhagavad Gita.

Chapter 2, Verse 47 states:

"Karmanye vadhikaraste ma phaleshu kadachana."

"You have a right to action alone, never to its fruits."

This verse does not discourage effort.

It encourages focus.

Do the work.
Perform your duty.
Act with integrity.

But do not become imprisoned by outcomes.

THE RETIREMENT APPLICATION

This principle applies directly to retirement.

We can save diligently.

We can care for our health.

We can strengthen relationships.

We can pursue learning.

We can travel.

We can serve others.

The results may not always unfold exactly as planned.

Yet the effort itself retains value.

THE PRACTICE OF MEDITATION

Meditation is one method of cultivating Spiritual Assets.

Meditation encourages observation rather than reaction.

It creates space between events and responses.

It often increases clarity, patience, and self-awareness.

Many retirees discover that a few quiet minutes each day produce benefits that extend far beyond the meditation session itself.

CASE STUDY

Imagine two retirees facing similar challenges.

One becomes overwhelmed by uncertainty.

The other draws upon spiritual practices, gratitude, and perspective.

The external circumstances may be identical.

The internal experience may be dramatically different.

Spiritual Assets influence how life is experienced.

THE GRATITUDE PRINCIPLE

Gratitude is one of the simplest and most powerful spiritual practices.

Gratitude shifts attention from scarcity to abundance.

From what is missing to what is present.

From fear to appreciation.

WORKSHEET

Spiritual Asset Inventory

What gives your life meaning?

What spiritual practices support you?

What lessons have life's challenges taught?

What are you most grateful for today?

How do you define dharma in your own life?

What actions strengthen your inner peace?

REFLECTION

Spiritual Assets may not appear on any balance sheet.

Yet they often determine whether life feels meaningful.

Financial wealth can improve comfort.

Spiritual wealth can improve perspective.

Together they create a more complete form of resilience.

For these reasons, Spiritual Assets deserve recognition as one of the most valuable invisible assets available to retirees.

Inner peace is a form of wealth.

Chapter 10 – Time Assets: The Most Democratic Asset

Every day, each of us receives the same deposit.

Twenty-four hours.

No one receives more.
No one receives less.

Billionaires receive twenty-four hours.
Students receive twenty-four hours.
Retirees receive twenty-four hours.

Time is the most democratic asset in existence.

Yet it is also one of the most misunderstood.

When I was younger, time often felt abundant.

There would always be another year.
Another opportunity.
Another season of life.

As I grew older, I began to understand that time is not merely a resource.

It is the resource from which all other experiences are created.

THE INVISIBLE NATURE OF TIME

Unlike money, time cannot be saved.

Unlike investments, it cannot compound in an account.

Unlike property, it cannot be transferred.

Once spent, it is gone forever.

This reality gives Time Assets unique importance.

THE RETIREMENT PARADOX

Many people spend decades accumulating financial assets in order to enjoy greater freedom later.

Retirement finally provides something that working years often restrict:

Discretionary time.

Yet many retirees discover an unexpected challenge.

They know how to earn money.

They never learned how to invest time.

THE TIME PORTFOLIO

Every retiree maintains a Time Portfolio.

The question is not whether you have one.

The question is how you allocate it.

Some common categories include:

- Health
- Relationships
- Learning
- Travel
- Service
- Recreation
- Reflection
- Creativity
- Spiritual Practice

The quality of a retirement often reflects the quality of these allocations.

MY OBSERVATION

Some of the happiest retirees I have met are intentional with time.

They maintain routines.

They pursue interests.

They cultivate relationships.

They continue learning.

Their calendars reflect their priorities.

Others drift from day to day.

The difference is rarely explained by money alone.

CASE STUDY

Imagine two retirees.

Retiree A has substantial financial resources but little structure.

Days blend together.

Months pass quickly.

Retiree B intentionally allocates time toward health, learning, relationships, service, and meaningful experiences.

Ten years later, the difference may be dramatic.

The second retiree has not merely spent time.

The second retiree has invested it.

THE MORTALITY FACTOR

Time becomes more valuable as we recognize its limits.

Retirement often brings increased awareness of mortality.

This awareness need not create fear.

Instead, it can create focus.

When time is recognized as finite, priorities become clearer.

The question shifts from:

"What do I want to own?"

to:

"How do I want to spend the time I have?"

THE TIME DIVIDEND

A wisely used hour produces benefits beyond the hour itself.

A walk improves health.

A conversation strengthens a relationship.

Reading expands knowledge.

Meditation increases clarity.

The hour ends.

The benefits remain.

WORKSHEET

Time Asset Inventory

How did you spend yesterday?

How much time was devoted to:

Health:
Relationships:
Learning:
Service:
Recreation:
Reflection:

Do your daily activities reflect your highest priorities?

What one change would improve your Time Portfolio?

THE GREATEST ASSET

Retirement planning often focuses on money.

Money matters.

But money exists to support life.

Time is life.

The purpose of financial assets is to create the freedom to use time well.

REFLECTION

Time may be the most valuable invisible asset because it is the asset from which all others are built.

Relationships require time.

Health requires time.

Knowledge requires time.

Travel requires time.

Spiritual growth requires time.

A meaningful retirement is ultimately a story about how time was used.

For these reasons, Time Assets deserve recognition as one of the most important invisible assets available to retirees.

The question is not how much time we have.

The question is how wisely we use it.

Chapter 11 – Freedom Assets: The Ability to Choose

If I were asked to identify the ultimate purpose of all the invisible assets discussed in this book,
my answer would be simple:

Freedom.

Not unlimited freedom.
Not freedom from responsibility.

Rather, the ability to make meaningful choices about how life is lived.

THE HIGHEST-LEVEL ASSET

As I developed the Invisible Assets framework, I gradually realized something important.

Social Security supports freedom.

Health supports freedom.

Relationships support freedom.

Knowledge supports freedom.

Experiences support freedom.

Travel supports freedom.

Spiritual perspective supports freedom.

Time supports freedom.

Freedom is not merely another invisible asset.

Freedom is the outcome produced by a healthy portfolio of invisible assets.

THE MANY DIMENSIONS OF FREEDOM

Freedom appears in many forms.

Financial Freedom.
Physical Freedom.
Emotional Freedom.
Intellectual Freedom.
Spiritual Freedom.
Geographic Freedom.
Time Freedom.

Each dimension influences quality of life.

A retiree with financial resources but poor health may experience limited physical freedom.

A healthy retiree burdened by financial stress may experience limited financial freedom.

A person with wealth but no purpose may experience limited emotional freedom.

True freedom often requires balance.

THE RETIREMENT QUESTION

Many people spend decades pursuing financial independence.

A more useful question may be:

What is the freedom I hope financial independence will create?

The answer differs for every person.

For some, freedom means travel.

For others, it means family.

For others, it means service, learning, creativity, or spiritual practice.

MY OBSERVATION

Throughout life I have noticed that people frequently pursue goals indirectly.

They seek money because they desire security.

They seek security because they desire freedom.

They seek freedom because they desire a meaningful life.

Understanding this progression helps clarify priorities.

CASE STUDY

Imagine two retirees.

Retiree A possesses substantial financial assets but feels trapped by anxiety, poor health, and lack of purpose.

Retiree B possesses fewer financial assets but enjoys good health, meaningful relationships, purpose, and sufficient income.

Who is truly freer?

The answer extends beyond balance sheets.

THE FREEDOM PORTFOLIO

Freedom Assets may include:

- Reliable income
- Functional health
- Strong relationships
- Knowledge and adaptability
- Meaningful experiences
- Travel opportunities
- Spiritual perspective
- Purpose
- Time flexibility

Together these create optionality.

Optionality creates freedom.

THE FREEDOM TEST

Consider the following questions.

Can you choose how to spend your time?

Can you pursue meaningful activities?

Can you maintain important relationships?

Can you continue learning?

Can you adapt to change?

Can you travel if desired?

Can you find peace during uncertainty?

The answers reveal the strength of your Freedom Assets.

WORKSHEET

Freedom Asset Inventory

What does freedom mean to you?

Which forms of freedom matter most?

Financial:
Physical:
Emotional:
Intellectual:
Spiritual:

Which area requires improvement?

What invisible asset would strengthen that area most?

THE PARADOX OF ENOUGH

One of the most important retirement questions is:

How much is enough?

There is no universal answer.

Yet many people discover that freedom depends less on maximizing everything and more on having enough.

Enough income.
Enough health.
Enough purpose.
Enough connection.

Enough to live deliberately.

REFLECTION

The purpose of retirement planning is not retirement itself.

The purpose is freedom.

The purpose of freedom is not comfort alone.

The purpose is the opportunity to live intentionally, serve others, continue growing, and experience life fully.

For these reasons, Freedom Assets deserve recognition as perhaps the most important invisible assets of all.

The Invisible Assets ultimately lead to one destination:

The freedom to live well.

Chapter 12 – The Hidden Portfolio

For most of my life, I believed a portfolio consisted of financial assets.

Stocks.
Bonds.
Cash.
Real estate.

If someone asked about my portfolio, those were the items I would have discussed.

Over time, however, I came to recognize a much larger reality.

Every person possesses two portfolios.

The Visible Portfolio and the Hidden Portfolio.

The Visible Portfolio appears on statements and spreadsheets.

The Hidden Portfolio exists largely outside of traditional accounting.

Yet it may be equally important.

Sometimes it may be more important.

THE DISCOVERY

The Invisible Assets discussed throughout this book gradually led me toward an important realization.

Social Security is part of a portfolio.

Health is part of a portfolio.

Relationships are part of a portfolio.

Knowledge is part of a portfolio.

Experiences are part of a portfolio.

Travel is part of a portfolio.

Spiritual perspective is part of a portfolio.

Time is part of a portfolio.

Freedom is part of a portfolio.

Viewed individually, these assets appear unrelated.

Viewed collectively, they form a powerful hidden portfolio.

THE LIMITATIONS OF NET WORTH

Net worth measures certain aspects of financial position.

It does not measure:

Purpose.
Meaning.

Resilience.
Health.
Wisdom.
Relationships.
Gratitude.

A person may possess a substantial net worth and still feel impoverished in important areas of life.

Conversely, someone with modest financial resources may possess extraordinary invisible wealth.

THE RETIREMENT BALANCE SHEET

Imagine creating a balance sheet that includes invisible assets.

Assets

Financial Assets
Social Security Assets
Health Assets
Relationship Assets
Knowledge Assets
Experience Assets
Travel Assets
Spiritual Assets
Time Assets
Freedom Assets

Liabilities

Poor Health
Isolation

Debt
Chronic Stress
Lack of Purpose
Fear
Inflexibility

The resulting picture may differ dramatically from a traditional financial statement.

CASE STUDY

Imagine two retirees.

Retiree A possesses a seven-figure investment portfolio but struggles with poor health, loneliness, and lack of purpose.

Retiree B possesses a smaller financial portfolio but enjoys good health, strong relationships, ongoing learning, meaningful activities, and spiritual balance.

Traditional accounting may favor Retiree A.

The Hidden Portfolio may favor Retiree B.

MY OBSERVATION

As I reflected on retirement, I realized that some of my most valuable assets could not be sold.

I could not sell my memories.

I could not sell my experiences.

I could not sell my relationships.

I could not sell my knowledge.

Yet these assets continued to produce value every day.

THE INTERACTION EFFECT

Invisible Assets rarely operate independently.

Health supports travel.

Travel expands knowledge.

Knowledge deepens perspective.

Perspective strengthens spiritual understanding.

Spiritual understanding improves resilience.

Resilience protects freedom.

The assets reinforce one another.

This interaction creates a multiplier effect.

WORKSHEET

Hidden Portfolio Assessment

Rate each category from 1 to 10.

Financial Assets:

Health Assets:
Relationship Assets:
Knowledge Assets:
Experience Assets:
Travel Assets:
Spiritual Assets:
Time Assets:
Freedom Assets:

Which category is strongest?

Which category requires the most attention?

What single improvement would strengthen your overall Hidden Portfolio most?

THE PORTFOLIO MANAGER

Every retiree serves as the manager of a Hidden Portfolio.

The responsibility cannot be delegated.

The decisions are personal.

The outcomes are cumulative.

Each day becomes an opportunity to strengthen one or more invisible assets.

REFLECTION

The purpose of this book is not simply to help readers build wealth.

Its purpose is to help readers recognize the full scope of their Hidden Portfolio.

Retirement success is rarely determined by a single asset.

Instead, it emerges from the interaction of many invisible assets working together.

The Hidden Portfolio is where those assets reside.

Understanding it may be one of the most important discoveries of retirement.

Chapter 13 – The COLA Surface Area Effect

When most people hear the phrase Cost-of-Living Adjustment, or COLA, they think about percentages.

Two percent.
Three percent.
Perhaps four percent.

The discussion usually ends there.

Over time, however, I began to view COLA differently.

I realized that the real power of COLA is not found in the percentage itself.

It is found in what that percentage acts upon.

I call this the COLA Surface Area Effect.

THE FOUNDATION PRINCIPLE

Imagine two retirees.

Retiree A receives $1,500 per month from an inflation-adjusted income source.

Retiree B receives $3,500 per month from an inflation-adjusted income source.

Both receive the same percentage increase.

Yet the larger base produces a larger dollar increase.

The percentage is identical.

The outcome is different.

The difference is the surface area.

A larger base creates a larger platform upon which future adjustments operate.

THE BIGGER BASE CONCEPT

Earlier in this book I discussed the idea of building a bigger base.

The COLA Surface Area Effect explains why that matters.

The larger the base, the larger the impact of each inflation adjustment.

This effect continues year after year.

The result is not merely higher income.

The result is increased resilience.

THE CONNECTION TO INVISIBLE ASSETS

At first glance, COLA appears to be a financial topic.

In reality, it affects many invisible assets.

A larger inflation-adjusted income stream may support:

- Health Assets
- Relationship Assets
- Travel Assets
- Knowledge Assets
- Spiritual Assets
- Freedom Assets

Financial resilience becomes a platform that supports other forms of resilience.

THE CANVAS ANALOGY

One of my favorite ways to think about retirement is through the idea of a canvas.

A larger canvas does not guarantee a better painting.

But it provides more room to create.

Similarly, a larger inflation-protected income base does not guarantee happiness.

Yet it often creates additional flexibility and options.

Options are valuable.

Options support freedom.

CASE STUDY

Imagine two retirees facing an inflationary period.

The first retiree relies primarily on fixed income that does not adjust.

The second retiree receives a meaningful inflation-adjusted income stream.

As prices rise, the experiences of the two retirees may diverge.

The second retiree may retain greater purchasing power and flexibility.

That flexibility helps preserve invisible assets.

THE RESILIENCE MULTIPLIER

The true value of COLA extends beyond dollars.

A larger inflation-adjusted income foundation may:

Reduce stress.

Support health.

Enable travel.

Protect independence.

Provide peace of mind.

These secondary effects are often overlooked.

Yet they may be more important than the additional

income itself.

WORKSHEET

COLA Surface Area Assessment

Current monthly inflation-adjusted income:

____

How does that income support:

Health?
Relationships?
Learning?
Travel?
Freedom?

If your inflation-adjusted income increased by 10%, what additional flexibility would it create?

What invisible assets would benefit most?

THE LONG VIEW

The COLA Surface Area Effect is not about maximizing every dollar.

It is about understanding how a larger inflation-protected foundation creates greater resilience over time.

The effect compounds slowly.

But retirement itself is a long-term endeavor.

Small differences repeated over many years often become significant.

REFLECTION

Many people focus on investment returns.

Returns matter.

Yet retirement resilience is also influenced by the quality and durability of income.

The COLA Surface Area Effect highlights an important truth:

A larger inflation-adjusted foundation can strengthen far more than finances.

It can strengthen the entire portfolio of Invisible Assets.

The percentage may be small.

The impact may be large.

Chapter 14 – Debt in Context

Debt is often discussed in absolute terms.

Debt is bad.
Debt is dangerous.
Debt must be eliminated at all costs.

There is truth in these warnings.

Yet retirement has taught me that reality is usually more nuanced.

Debt exists within context.

Understanding that context is essential.

THE INVISIBLE ASSETS PERSPECTIVE

Traditional financial discussions often evaluate debt primarily through numbers.

Balance.
Interest rate.
Monthly payment.

These measurements matter.

But debt also affects invisible assets.

Debt can influence:

Freedom.
Stress.
Health.
Relationships.
Time.
Flexibility.

The true impact of debt extends beyond mathematics.

DEBT AS A CLAIM ON THE FUTURE

Every debt obligation represents a future claim on resources.

Future income.

Future cash flow.

Future choices.

This is one reason debt influences freedom.

The larger the obligation, the fewer options may remain available.

THE STRESS FACTOR

Not all debt creates the same emotional burden.

Some people carry modest debt comfortably.

Others experience significant stress from relatively small balances.

The emotional component matters.

Stress affects health.

Health affects resilience.

Resilience affects the Hidden Portfolio.

Everything is connected.

CASE STUDY

Imagine two retirees.

Retiree A has no debt but also no financial flexibility.

Retiree B carries modest debt but possesses reliable income, strong cash flow, and a clear repayment strategy.

Which retiree is in the stronger position?

The answer depends upon context.

Debt cannot be evaluated in isolation.

THE DEBT SPECTRUM

Debt exists on a spectrum.

At one end:

Manageable debt supported by reliable cash flow.

At the other:

Debt that creates chronic stress and threatens stability.

The objective is not merely to reach zero.

The objective is to increase resilience.

MY OBSERVATION

Many financial discussions focus entirely on elimination.

While reducing debt is often wise, the larger question is:

How does debt affect the Invisible Assets?

Does it reduce freedom?

Does it increase anxiety?

Does it limit opportunities?

Does it interfere with health or relationships?

Those questions often matter more than the balance itself.

THE FREEDOM CONNECTION

Debt is important because it competes with freedom.

Every payment directs resources toward past decisions rather than future choices.

Reducing debt may create:

More flexibility.
More security.
More options.
Less stress.

In many cases, the greatest benefit is psychological rather than financial.

THE RESILIENCE TEST

A useful question is:

Could I comfortably manage this debt during an unexpected challenge?

If the answer is yes, resilience remains intact.

If the answer is no, additional attention may be warranted.

WORKSHEET

Debt Context Assessment

Current Debt Categories:

Mortgage:
Vehicle:
Credit Cards:
Personal Loans:
Other:

How much stress does each obligation create?

Rate from 1 to 10.

Which debt most affects your sense of freedom?

What repayment strategy would strengthen your Hidden Portfolio most?

What would life look like with that obligation reduced or eliminated?

THE GOAL

The objective is not perfection.

The objective is progress.

Small improvements compound over time.

Each reduction in debt may increase freedom, flexibility, and peace of mind.

REFLECTION

Debt is not merely a financial issue.

It is a resilience issue.

It influences many Invisible Assets simultaneously.

The healthiest approach is neither panic nor denial.

It is thoughtful management.

Retirement resilience grows when debt occupies a smaller portion of life and freedom occupies a larger one.

Viewed through the lens of Invisible Assets, debt is best understood not as an isolated liability but as a factor that affects the entire Hidden Portfolio.

Chapter 15 – The Churn Principle: Reducing Friction, Preserving Energy

As I reflected on retirement, I noticed a pattern that traditional financial planning rarely addresses.

Many people are not defeated by a lack of resources.

They are exhausted by unnecessary churn.

I began referring to this phenomenon as The Churn Principle.

Churn is the constant expenditure of energy, attention, money, and time on activities that produce little meaningful progress.

THE MANY FORMS OF CHURN

Most people immediately think of financial churn.

Unnecessary fees.
Poor purchasing decisions.
Repeated financial mistakes.

Financial churn certainly exists.

But retirement revealed that churn appears in many

forms.

Time Churn.
Emotional Churn.
Relationship Churn.
Decision Churn.
Information Churn.
Health Churn.

Each type consumes resources that could be directed toward more meaningful purposes.

THE ENERGY ECONOMY

Every person operates within an Energy Economy.

Energy is finite.

Attention is finite.

Time is finite.

The older I became, the more valuable these resources appeared.

I realized that reducing unnecessary churn often created greater benefits than increasing effort.

THE RETIREMENT ADVANTAGE

Retirement provides an opportunity to redesign life.

Many routines that once served a purpose can be reexamined.

Some commitments can be simplified.

Some obligations can be eliminated.

Some worries can be released.

The result is often greater freedom with less effort.

CASE STUDY

Imagine two retirees.

Retiree A constantly reacts to every news cycle, every market fluctuation, every minor problem, and every source of stress.

Retiree B focuses attention on health, relationships, learning, purpose, and meaningful activities.

Both experience challenges.

Yet the second retiree preserves more energy for what matters.

The difference is churn.

DECISION FATIGUE

One of the least recognized forms of churn is decision fatigue.

Every unnecessary decision consumes mental energy.

Simplified routines reduce this burden.

Many successful people intentionally simplify aspects of life.

The objective is not rigidity.

The objective is preserving attention for important decisions.

HEALTH CHURN

Health churn appears when preventable problems repeatedly consume time and energy.

Poor sleep.
Poor nutrition.
Lack of movement.
Excessive stress.

Small improvements often reduce future churn dramatically.

RELATIONSHIP CHURN

Not every relationship contributes equally to well-being.

Some relationships create encouragement and growth.

Others generate constant conflict and exhaustion.

Recognizing this difference is important.

Protecting Relationship Assets sometimes requires

reducing unnecessary relationship churn.

THE CHURN AUDIT

One useful exercise is conducting a Churn Audit.

Ask:

What repeatedly consumes time without creating value?

What repeatedly consumes energy without creating progress?

What repeatedly creates stress without producing growth?

The answers often reveal opportunities for simplification.

WORKSHEET

Personal Churn Assessment

Rate each area from 1 to 10.

Financial Churn:
Time Churn:
Emotional Churn:
Relationship Churn:
Health Churn:
Information Churn:

Which area creates the greatest drain?

What one change would reduce that drain most

effectively?

THE MULTIPLIER EFFECT

Reducing churn creates a multiplier effect.

More energy.

More attention.

More time.

More clarity.

These resources become available to strengthen Invisible Assets.

Health improves.

Relationships improve.

Learning improves.

Freedom expands.

MY OBSERVATION

Many people focus exclusively on accumulation.

Earn more.
Save more.
Own more.

Accumulation matters.

But retirement taught me another lesson:

Sometimes the most effective strategy is subtraction.

Remove friction.

Remove clutter.

Remove unnecessary obligations.

Remove recurring drains.

The resulting freedom often exceeds expectations.

REFLECTION

The Churn Principle is ultimately about stewardship.

It encourages thoughtful management of attention, energy, and time.

Every reduction in unnecessary churn strengthens the Hidden Portfolio.

Retirement resilience is not only about what we add.

It is also about what we eliminate.

When friction decreases, Invisible Assets flourish.

That is the essence of the Churn Principle.

Chapter 16 – Lifelong Resilience: The True Objective of Retirement Planning

If I were asked to summarize this entire book in a single word, that word would be resilience.

Not wealth.

Not retirement.

Not even freedom.

Resilience.

Because resilience determines how well we navigate both expected and unexpected challenges.

The Invisible Assets framework ultimately exists for one purpose:

To build resilience.

THE LIMITATION OF TRADITIONAL PLANNING

Traditional retirement planning often focuses on accumulation.

How much money do I need?

How much should I save?

What return should I expect?

These questions matter.

Yet life repeatedly demonstrates that retirement success depends on more than numbers.

Unexpected health events occur.

Relationships change.

Markets fluctuate.

Inflation rises.

Circumstances evolve.

Resilience determines how effectively we respond.

THE RESILIENCE PORTFOLIO

Throughout this book we have explored a variety of Invisible Assets.

Social Security Assets.
Health Assets.
Relationship Assets.
Knowledge Assets.
Experience Assets.
Travel Assets.
Spiritual Assets.

Time Assets.
Freedom Assets.

Viewed together, they create a Resilience Portfolio.

Each asset contributes differently.

Some provide stability.

Some provide flexibility.

Some provide perspective.

Together they increase adaptability.

THE BAMBOO PRINCIPLE

I often think of resilience through the image of bamboo.

Strong winds may bend bamboo.

Yet bamboo often survives because it remains flexible.

Rigid structures sometimes break.

Flexible structures often endure.

Retirement resilience works similarly.

The objective is not to eliminate every challenge.

The objective is to remain capable of adapting.

CASE STUDY

Imagine two retirees.

Retiree A possesses significant financial wealth but limited adaptability.

Unexpected challenges create substantial disruption.

Retiree B possesses a balanced portfolio of Invisible Assets.

Health.
Relationships.
Knowledge.
Purpose.
Reliable income.

When difficulties arise, these assets provide support.

The second retiree is not immune to challenges.

The second retiree is better prepared to navigate them.

THE RESILIENCE MULTIPLIER

One of the most interesting characteristics of resilience is that it compounds.

Improved health supports learning.

Learning supports adaptability.

Adaptability supports confidence.

Confidence supports action.

Action strengthens resilience further.

The assets reinforce one another.

THE ROLE OF PURPOSE

Purpose is often overlooked in retirement discussions.

Yet purpose acts as a stabilizing force.

People with purpose frequently demonstrate greater persistence during adversity.

Purpose provides direction.

Direction provides momentum.

Momentum supports resilience.

THE RESILIENCE QUESTIONS

When evaluating retirement readiness, consider the following questions:

Can I adapt to change?

Can I recover from setbacks?

Can I maintain meaningful relationships?

Can I continue learning?

Can I preserve health and mobility?

Can I find purpose during uncertainty?

Can I remain hopeful during challenges?

The answers reveal resilience more clearly than many financial calculations.

WORKSHEET

Personal Resilience Assessment

Rate yourself from 1 to 10.

Adaptability:
Health:
Relationships:
Purpose:
Learning:
Spiritual Perspective:
Financial Stability:
Optimism:

Which area is strongest?

Which area requires improvement?

What one action would strengthen your resilience most?

THE LONG VIEW

Retirement is not a destination.

It is a season of life.

Like every season, it contains opportunities and challenges.

The objective is not perfection.

The objective is preparation.

Preparedness increases confidence.

Confidence increases resilience.

MY OBSERVATION

Some of the most resilient people I have met are not necessarily the wealthiest.

They possess balance.

Perspective.

Adaptability.

Gratitude.

Purpose.

They understand that true security comes from more than money alone.

REFLECTION

The Invisible Assets framework began with a simple

observation:

Many of life's most valuable assets do not appear on financial statements.

As the framework expanded, a larger truth emerged.

Those assets are important because they create resilience.

Resilience protects freedom.

Resilience preserves meaning.

Resilience supports a life well lived.

For these reasons, lifelong resilience may be the ultimate objective of retirement planning.

Everything else is preparation.

Chapter 17 – Bhagavad Gita 2.47 and Retirement: Action, Equanimity, and a Life Well Lived

Of all the ideas explored in this book, none has influenced my thinking more deeply than a single verse from the Bhagavad Gita.

Bhagavad Gita 2.47 states:

कर्मण्येवाधिकारस्ते मा फलेषु कदाचन ।

मा कर्मफलहेतुर्भूर्मा ते सङ्गोऽस्त्वकर्मणि

॥

Transliteration:

Karmanye vadhikaraste ma phaleshu kadachana;
Ma karma-phala-hetur bhur ma te sango'stv akarmani.

Translation:

You have a right to action alone, never to its fruits. Let not the fruits of action be your motive, nor let your attachment be to inaction.

At first glance, this teaching may appear unrelated to retirement planning.

Over time, however, I came to see that it may be one of the most practical retirement principles ever expressed.

THE OUTCOME TRAP

Much of modern life revolves around outcomes.

Promotions.
Investment returns.
Net worth.
Status.
Recognition.

Outcomes matter.

Yet outcomes are never completely under our control.

Effort is under our control.

Integrity is under our control.

Preparation is under our control.

Action is under our control.

The Gita encourages us to focus attention where influence actually exists.

THE RETIREMENT APPLICATION

Retirement planning illustrates this principle perfectly.

We can save diligently.

We can invest responsibly.

We can maintain our health.

We can strengthen relationships.

We can continue learning.

We can pursue purpose.

Yet we cannot control every future event.

Markets fluctuate.

Inflation changes.

Health circumstances evolve.

Life remains uncertain.

The Gita does not promise certainty.

It teaches how to live wisely despite uncertainty.

MY OBSERVATION

One of the most liberating realizations of my retirement journey was understanding that success and peace of mind are not identical.

A person may achieve impressive outcomes and still remain anxious.

Another may experience setbacks yet remain peaceful.

The difference often lies in perspective.

THE INVISIBLE ASSETS CONNECTION

Every Invisible Asset discussed in this book requires action.

Health Assets require action.

Relationship Assets require action.

Knowledge Assets require action.

Spiritual Assets require action.

Freedom Assets require action.

The Gita provides a framework for cultivating these assets without becoming consumed by outcomes.

THE PARADOX OF EQUANIMITY

Equanimity does not mean passivity.

Equanimity does not mean indifference.

Equanimity means maintaining balance regardless of outcomes.

Continue acting.

Continue learning.

Continue serving.

Continue growing.

But avoid allowing external results to determine inner peace.

CASE STUDY

Imagine two retirees.

Both experience an unexpected setback.

The first becomes overwhelmed by disappointment.

The second acknowledges the challenge, adapts, and continues moving forward.

The external event is identical.

The internal response differs.

The Gita focuses on that internal response.

DHARMA IN RETIREMENT

The concept of dharma is often misunderstood.

Dharma is not merely obligation.

Dharma is right action.

Purposeful action.

Responsible action.

Retirement does not eliminate dharma.

It changes its expression.

The opportunity to contribute remains.

The opportunity to learn remains.

The opportunity to serve remains.

The opportunity to grow remains.

WORKSHEET

Reflection on Gita 2.47

What actions are fully within my control?

Which outcomes create unnecessary anxiety?

How would my life change if I focused more on effort than results?

What is my dharma in this season of life?

How can I act more deliberately while remaining less attached to outcomes?

THE FREEDOM OF RIGHT ACTION

One of the greatest gifts of this verse is freedom.

When attention shifts from outcomes to action, anxiety often decreases.

Energy becomes available for growth.

Effort becomes its own reward.

The process becomes meaningful.

MY PERSONAL CONCLUSION

As I reflected upon retirement, I realized that the purpose of planning was never to guarantee perfect outcomes.

Such guarantees do not exist.

The purpose was to prepare thoughtfully, act responsibly, and then live fully.

That is precisely what Bhagavad Gita 2.47 teaches.

REFLECTION

The Invisible Assets framework ultimately supports a simple objective:

Live well.

Act wisely.

Serve where possible.

Continue growing.

Accept uncertainty.

Preserve equanimity.

Bhagavad Gita 2.47 provides a timeless foundation for this approach.

It reminds us that while outcomes remain uncertain, meaningful action is always available.

That may be one of the most valuable invisible assets of all.

Chapter 18 – Building a Personal Retirement Constitution

Every nation has a constitution.

Organizations often have mission statements.

Successful businesses operate according to guiding principles.

Yet many people move through retirement without a clearly defined framework for decision-making.

Over time, I realized that retirement benefits from its own constitution.

Not a legal document.

A personal document.

A statement of principles.

A declaration of values.

A guide for action.

I call this a Personal Retirement Constitution.

WHY A CONSTITUTION MATTERS

Life presents endless decisions.

How should I spend my time?

What deserves my attention?

What is enough?

What do I value most?

Without a framework, decisions often become reactive.

A constitution creates consistency.

It provides direction during uncertainty.

It helps align actions with values.

THE INVISIBLE ASSETS FOUNDATION

My Personal Retirement Constitution emerged naturally from the Invisible Assets framework.

As I reflected on retirement, several priorities became clear.

Health matters.

Relationships matter.

Learning matters.

Purpose matters.

Freedom matters.

Spiritual growth matters.

Resilience matters.

These priorities became guiding principles.

THE DIFFERENCE BETWEEN GOALS AND PRINCIPLES

Goals are important.

Yet goals change.

Principles endure.

A goal may be to visit a specific destination.

A principle may be to remain curious and continue exploring.

A goal may be to eliminate debt.

A principle may be to preserve freedom and reduce unnecessary burdens.

Principles provide long-term guidance.

THE RETIREMENT CONSTITUTION TEMPLATE

Article I – Health

I will treat health as one of my most valuable invisible

assets.

I will support physical, mental, and emotional well-being through consistent actions.

Article II – Relationships

I will invest time and energy in meaningful relationships.

I will value connection above accumulation.

Article III – Learning

I will remain a lifelong student.

I will continue expanding knowledge, perspective, and understanding.

Article IV – Purpose

I will seek meaningful activities that contribute to personal growth and service.

Article V – Freedom

I will make decisions that strengthen long-term freedom rather than reduce it.

Article VI – Resilience

I will prepare thoughtfully for challenges while remaining adaptable.

Article VII – Spiritual Perspective

I will cultivate gratitude, reflection, and inner peace.

Article VIII – Action

I will focus on actions within my control and accept uncertainty regarding outcomes.

THE GITA CONNECTION

This final article reflects Bhagavad Gita 2.47.

Act wisely.

Act consistently.

Act responsibly.

Then release attachment to outcomes.

This principle belongs in any Personal Retirement Constitution.

CASE STUDY

Imagine two retirees.

The first reacts to circumstances as they arise.

The second possesses a clear set of principles.

Both encounter challenges.

Yet the second retiree often experiences greater clarity

because important decisions are filtered through established values.

The constitution becomes a compass.

THE REVIEW PROCESS

A constitution should not remain hidden in a drawer.

It should be reviewed regularly.

Values evolve.

Priorities change.

New insights emerge.

Periodic review keeps the document relevant.

WORKSHEET

Draft Your Personal Retirement Constitution

What values matter most?

What invisible assets deserve protection?

What principles guide your decisions?

What forms of freedom are most important?

How do you define a life well lived?

What legacy would you like to leave?

Write five personal articles for your constitution.

1.

2.

3.

4.

5.

MY OBSERVATION

The most fulfilled retirees I have met often possess a clear sense of direction.

Not because life is predictable.

Because their values are clear.

Clarity simplifies decisions.

Clarity reduces churn.

Clarity supports resilience.

REFLECTION

A Personal Retirement Constitution is ultimately a declaration of intentional living.

It transforms retirement from a collection of activities into a coherent philosophy.

The Invisible Assets framework provides the building blocks.

The Personal Retirement Constitution assembles those blocks into a structure.

A life guided by clear principles is more likely to remain resilient, meaningful, and free.

That is why every retiree should consider creating one.

The Invisible Assets are valuable.

A constitution helps ensure they are used wisely.

Epilogue – Preserve Freedom

As I reach the end of this book, I find myself returning to a single idea.

Preserve freedom.

Throughout these pages we explored many Invisible Assets.

Social Security.
Health.
Relationships.
Knowledge.
Experiences.
Travel.
Spiritual perspective.
Time.
Freedom.
Resilience.

Each asset contributes something valuable.

Yet together they point toward a larger objective.

The ability to live deliberately.

The ability to make meaningful choices.

The ability to continue growing.

The ability to serve, learn, explore, and appreciate life.

In other words:

Freedom.

THE JOURNEY

When I first began thinking about retirement, I viewed it primarily as a financial milestone.

Over time that perspective expanded.

Retirement became less about reaching a number and more about creating a life.

A life supported by many forms of wealth.

Some visible.

Some invisible.

The Invisible Assets framework emerged from that realization.

THE BALANCE

No single asset guarantees fulfillment.

Financial wealth alone is not enough.

Health alone is not enough.

Relationships alone are not enough.

The most resilient retirements often emerge from balance.

A balanced Hidden Portfolio.

A balanced life.

A balanced perspective.

THE ROLE OF ACTION

One lesson appears repeatedly throughout this book.

Meaningful outcomes begin with meaningful actions.

Health improves through daily habits.

Relationships strengthen through attention.

Knowledge grows through curiosity.

Freedom expands through thoughtful choices.

The process matters.

Small actions accumulate.

THE GITA REMINDER

Bhagavad Gita 2.47 teaches us to focus on action rather than attachment to outcomes.

This principle applies beautifully to retirement.

We cannot control every future event.

We cannot eliminate uncertainty.

We can prepare.

We can learn.

We can act.

We can remain adaptable.

We can preserve perspective.

These actions remain available regardless of circumstances.

THE TRUE MEASURE OF WEALTH

The longer I reflected on retirement, the more my definition of wealth evolved.

Wealth includes money.

But wealth also includes:

Health.

Purpose.

Friendship.

Wisdom.

Gratitude.

Time.

Freedom.

A person rich in these assets possesses a form of wealth that cannot easily be measured.

Yet it may be among the most valuable forms of wealth available.

A FINAL EXERCISE

Before closing this book, pause and consider the following questions.

Which Invisible Asset is strongest in your life?

Which Invisible Asset requires greater attention?

What action can you take this week to strengthen it?

What does freedom mean to you?

How will you preserve it?

MY HOPE FOR READERS

I do not expect every reader to agree with every idea in this book.

That is not the objective.

My hope is simpler.

I hope readers begin noticing the Invisible Assets already present within their lives.

I hope they strengthen those assets.

I hope they recognize that retirement can be richer, broader, and more meaningful than traditional financial discussions often suggest.

Most of all, I hope they preserve freedom.

Because freedom creates space for learning.

Freedom creates space for service.

Freedom creates space for gratitude.

Freedom creates space for life itself.

FINAL THOUGHT

The Invisible Assets are not hidden because they are rare.

They are hidden because they are often overlooked.

Once recognized, they can be cultivated.

Once cultivated, they can be protected.

Once protected, they can support a life of resilience,

meaning, and freedom.

That is the journey explored in this book.

May your own journey continue to expand the invisible assets that matter most.

And may you always preserve freedom.

www.ingramcontent.com/pod-product-compliance
Lightning Source LLC
LaVergne TN
LVHW022107200926
848481LV00003B/1091
9798993019871